GET THE INTERVIEW

&

GET THE JOB!

Insider Tips from a Human Resources Veteran!

By: Monica Boitnott

Copyright © 2020 by Monica Boitnott

All rights reserved. The use of any part of this publication reproduced, transmitted by any form or by any means, electronic, mechanical, photocopying, recording, or otherwise, or stored in a retrieval system, without the prior consent of the publisher or author is an infringement of the copyright law.

DISCLAIMER: The advice and strategies found within this work may not be suitable or successful in every situation. This work is sold with the understanding that neither the author nor the publisher is held responsible for the results accrued from the advice in this book. The intent of this work is to assist the individual who chooses to follow its recommendations in putting his/her best foot forward to enhance the possibility of a successful outcome.

TABLE OF CONTENTS

	Page #
Introduction	5
Chapter One - Your Resume	7

- Format
- Readability
- Content
- Professionalism

Chapter Two - You got the Interview! Now what?	15

- Preparing for the interview.
- Brainstorm Practice Questions.
- Preparing for the Specific Type of Interview:
    - Telephone
    - Video
    - In-Person

Chapter Three - The 3 C's of Interviewing	23

- Be Confident.
- Be Courteous.
- Be Concise.

Chapter Four - After the interview	27

- Immediate "To Do".
- Follow Up.

Conclusion	29
About the Author	31

INTRODUCTION

After 20 years in Human Resources, to say that I have seen the good, the bad and the ugly when it comes to resumes and interviews, is an understatement.

Over the years, I lost count of the number of times I uttered "What were they thinking?" under my breath after reading a resume or following an interview. Out of many cringe-worthy encounters blossomed the idea for this "how to" book.

Upon reading some portions of this work (such as the importance of dressing professionally for an interview), I anticipate hearing a reverberating "Well, duh!!" come from some of you. Trust me, however, based on personal experience, this is not a given for all. Each and every topic I address within the following pages exists because I have seen a need at some point in my career.

Regardless of whether you are a beginner or an old pro at the process, I write these pages with the sincere hope that those who read them find them beneficial and land the job of their dreams! And maybe…just maybe…you'll enjoy a chuckle or two along the way.

So, let's get moving!

"The secret of getting ahead is getting started."
– Mark Twain.

CHAPTER ONE

Your Resume

Remember…First impressions can make or break you! When it comes to landing that perfect job, your first opportunity to make a killer impression is typically through your resume.

That initial impression can mean an immediate rejection or a step closer to an interview. To understand just how critical this is, let me give you a peek behind the curtain into how the candidate selection process often works. Although the Hiring Manager is sometimes the first person to review your resume, frequently, this is not the case. Often, a Recruiter is the first hurdle that you have to get passed, and they may be weeding through literally hundreds of resumes all of which have been submitted for the job that you want. Thus, making a great first impression and ensuring your resume stands out as a great fit for the role is of utmost importance.

Why did I include this section? Recently, I was assisting an organization in filling several vacancies and for one job posting, they received almost 1,000 applications.

How do you make that great first impression?
- Format
- Readability
- Content
- Professionalism

Format:

If you're new to the job search arena and don't yet have a resume, you may be thinking, "I have no idea where to start." No problem. Templates and sample resumes are readily available on the internet. Also, if you're using Microsoft Word®, there are a variety of templates already set up from which to choose. *(Just open Word, select "New" and click on "Resumes and Cover Letters" or type "Resume" in the template search box.)* You can also search for resume templates and samples using any internet search engines.

You'll quickly see that there are many different options, so which format do you choose? The short answer is…it doesn't matter. Whichever template that appeals to you will work. My only recommendation is that you think about readability (more on this later) and the type of company and/or job for which you are applying in choosing your template. For example, is the role you are applying for with a more conservative, formal company or is it a new, trendy start-up and you're applying for a creative-type role? Selecting a format that aligns with the type of role you're seeking may be a good place to start in narrowing the field. In general, however, your resume template style is up to you.

Another question I often hear is…should I include my photo on the resume and/or other personal information? It seems that resume formats that include a photo are more prevalent than they use to be; mostly in technology and creative-type roles from what I have experienced. Again, however, this is up to you. If you do decide to include a photo on your resume, ensure it is a professional photo and presents you well (i.e., not one showing you out at the bar whooping it up with your friends, etc.). Let the company learn what a fun person you are after they hire you.

Why did I include this section? I actually reviewed a resume recently where the applicant had included a photo of her feet on her resume. No other photo, no explanation; just a photo of her feet. Definitely one of those "what was she thinking?" moments.

Readability:

What do I mean by Readability? Specifically, you want to ensure that the person making that initial call about whether or not to move your resume forward in the review/interview process can easily and quickly see that you meet the qualifications for the role. Remember what I said previously, Recruiters or Hiring Managers often have to weed through hundreds of resumes for a single job. They need to do this quickly and efficiently, and if they can't determine that you are a potential fit for the role within a matter of seconds, they will likely assume you are not and move on to the next applicant.

In thinking about Readability, there are 5-6 things you want to ensure are clear and easily identifiable:

- Your education (including certifications, if applicable);
- Current/previous employers;
- Dates of employment at each employer;
- Job title at each employer;
- Responsibilities/accomplishments in each job; and
- Software, computer systems, etc. that you've utilized (if applicable to the role to which you are applying).

I highly recommend the use of bullet points as I have done in the list above to improve Readability versus writing out your experience and responsibilities in a lengthy paragraph. For example, which below is easier to read and quickly determine the individual's experience and qualifications?

- *At this employer, I acted as the front desk receptionist and office manager. I was responsible for greeting visitors who came into the office and escorting them to the appropriate office. I also answered the telephone, took messages and scheduled appointments as needed. In addition, I typed correspondence for various managers as well as maintained their on-line calendars and booked travel as needed. Once a month, I would order office supplies to ensure we did not run out of any necessary items.*

    OR

- *Responsibilities included:*
    - *Greeted visitors and directed them to appropriate areas.*
    - *Answered the telephone, took messages & scheduled appointments.*
    - *Typed correspondence for various managers.*
    - *Maintained daily calendars for managers.*
    - *Booked travel as needed.*
    - *Placed monthly office supply order.*

Why did I include this section? I once received a 6-page resume in which every page was single-spaced top to bottom with paragraph after paragraph. The only breaks were where the candidate had placed the name of each previous employer in bold. Ugh!!! It was exhausting to look at it and a nightmare to read.

Content:
By content, I'm referencing all of the information that tells the prospective employer about you. This includes everything from your name and contact information to your education, qualifications and experiences.

It should go without saying that you should never, ever lie on your resume. The truth will come out either during the interview, the background check or, if you get hired, in your job performance. You do, however, want to put your best foot forward. Thus, I do not recommend including any negatives on your resume. For example, if you were fired from a previous job, there is no need to include this on your resume. If asked during the application or interview process, be truthful and use that opportunity to explain what happened and what you would do differently in the future.

Read the job description for the role to which you are applying. I can't stress this enough. If you have specific experience that matches the duties and responsibilities of the job, ensure these are included on your resume. Obviously, it's impossible to include every task you've ever done (nor would you want to); however, be sure to include experience that specifically matches that for which the employer is looking. As I shared above, often a Recruiter may be the first person to review your resume, and although most recruiters work hard to clearly understand the roles that they are hired to fill, in some cases, the only thing they have to go on is the job description. Thus, ensuring that your resume clearly reflects that your prior experience matches that in the job description can make it quick and easy for them to see that you're a potential match and immediately move you to the "yes" pile. NOTE: It's okay to have different versions of your resume for different employers as long as all details are truthful. Just keep track of which resume you've sent to which employer so when you get called for an interview, you'll know which one the interviewer is referencing.

There is much debate about how long a resume should be. For years, I've heard that the ideal length is no more than two (2) pages. Two pages is fine if you can adequately cover your experience and qualifications in that space. Personally, I feel that up to three (3) or even four (4) pages is okay if the space is needed to adequately reflect your experience and why you are a good fit for the role. However, as I mentioned previously, be as concise as possible while still getting your point across. It should be a rare instance in which a candidate needs to exceed four (4) pages for his/her resume; however, there are exceptions. Resumes for a Professor or Scientist, for example, who needs to highlight numerous conferences at which he/she has spoken, articles or research studies published, etc. may require a lengthier resume.

As for including personal information such as age, marital status, number of children, etc. on your resume, my recommendation is no. All of these are protected classes under Federal and/or State law; and thus, should not impact your ability to get hired; however, in my opinion, it just isn't necessary to include them on a resume. It's not relevant to your qualifications for the role to which you are applying, so leave it off.

Why did I include this section? I have, on more than one occasion, received resumes which I initially rejected as they did not appear to meet the minimum experience or qualifications for the role only to find out later that the candidate's experience did indeed match the job description. Unfortunately, he/she had prepared a generic, one-size fits all resume which did not include their experience that related to that specific job.

Professionalism:

Read your resume!! *Let me repeat that.* **READ** your resume!! Do **NOT** rely on spell check!

Spell check is wonderful and can certainly help clean up most typos; however, it cannot catch every error. For example, spell check may not catch "their" if you meant to type "there" as both are perfectly legitimate words just with different meanings. I highly recommend having a friend or family member proofread your resume as well. A fresh set of eyes is always good and can potentially point out not only spelling errors but grammar or readability issues.

Why did I include this section? Over the years, I have lost count of the number of resumes I have seen that included spelling errors. Believe it or not, I have received resumes in which candidates misspelled their own names or misspelled their current or previous job title…instead of a Production Manager, they were a Production Manger, for example. Remember, your resume is your first impression. Is your first impression going to be that of someone who is sloppy and doesn't care or that of someone who is professional with great attention to detail?

CHAPTER TWO

You Got the Interview! Now what?

You got the call! Your resume made a great impression and the potential new Employer has reached out to schedule an interview. Once you stop screaming with excitement and jumping up and down, it's time to get down to business.

Preparing for the Interview:
There are several things you should consider to ensure you're ready for your interview. The Company has a positive impression of you so far and you want to ensure that positive impression continues throughout the interview process. Thus, you'll want to consider and/or prep for the following:

- Brainstorm practice questions.
- Have specific examples ready.
- If it's a telephone or video interview, consider your environment.
- If it's an in-person interview, consider travel time/directions, what to bring, etc.

Brainstorm Practice Questions:
Although there is no way you can know exactly what the interviewer will ask, it's a good idea to brainstorm some practice questions and answers in advance so that you have responses in mind. This can help if you're one of those people whose mind goes blank when their nerves get the best of them. Even if they don't ask the exact question you've practiced, they may ask something very similar and you'll have a response ready to go. Remember, your answers should be professional and

thorough but concise and to the point. Some potential practice questions might include:

- Tell me about yourself.
- Walk me through your resume including why you decided to leave each employer.
- Why are you interested in this particular job?
- Why are you interested in this Company?
- What was it about the job posting that made you want to apply?
- What would your previous Manager or Supervisor say about you?
- What are you most proud of?
- What are your greatest strengths?
- What are your weaknesses?
- Why should we select you for this role over other candidates?
- If you could change something about your last job to make it better, what would you change?
- What salary or hourly rate are you seeking?

Also, many employers use behavior-based interview questions which require you to describe a situation, how you handled it and what was the result. Sample behavior-based questions might include:

- Tell me about a time when you were given a deadline and had trouble meeting it.
- Describe a situation in which you had difficulty getting along with a co-worker.
- Tell me about a time when you worked for a particularly difficult Manager or Supervisor.
- Give me an example of something you failed at and what you learned from it.

- Give me an example of something you did that was a huge success.
- (For Management/Supervisory roles) If you had an employee who was not performing as expected, how would you handle the situation?
- Give me an example of a recommendation you made on how to improve something about your job, work area, etc.

In addition to being prepared for questions the interviewer might ask you, ensure you have a few questions readily available to ask them as well. Toward the end of the interview, most interviewers will ask if you have any questions for them. Have a few in your hip pocket and ready to go.

Some questions, such as "How much does the job pay?" aren't usually a good question for the first interview. One exception to this might be if you're speaking to someone about a job and there is a question as to whether your experience far exceeds that required of the role (i.e., you're overqualified) and thus, you know you're looking for a salary to match your years of experience versus what has been described in the job description or during the interview. Just be thoughtful about how you approach the subject. For example, rather than saying something like, "Well, I have 10 years of experience, so I won't accept less than $30 per hour. Are you willing to pay me that much for this job?" You could instead ease into it with something like: "I realize this may not be an appropriate topic for a first interview; however, this role seems to require less experience than I currently have. I don't want to waste your time or mine and was just wondering if you would mind sharing the potential salary range for the role?" The interviewer will most likely appreciate you not wanting to waste his/her time and will respect you approaching the subject in such a professional manner. Be prepared, however, in case they turn the tables on you and instead of sharing their pay range, ask you how much you're seeking. Some companies openly share pay ranges for their jobs while others keep them close to the vest.

Unless you have a situation like I've described above, however, I would stay away from initiating the salary question. Even though we all want to make money (and as much of it as we can), Companies prefer to think that you want to be part of their team for reasons other than just cash.

You'll want to ensure that your questions are appropriate for the job to which you are applying. Some possible questions that you could ask at the end of the first interview might be:

- What are the next steps in the interview process?
- How would you describe the culture of your Company?
- How soon are you looking to fill the role?
- Is this a new role or a replacement?
- What does your initial training process for new hires look like?
- Can you share any information about the benefits you offer?
- When should I expect to hear back regarding whether or not I am being moved forward in the interview process?

Also, ensure you don't go on and on asking question after question. Normally, when the interviewer is ready to wrap up the interview …they're ready to wrap up the interview, so you don't want to annoy them. Unless you have a very specific reason for needing to ask additional questions, I recommend limiting it to 1-2 questions. Other questions can be asked at future interviews.

Preparing for the specific type of interview (i.e., Telephone, Video or In-Person):

Telephone Interview – Ensure you have cleared your calendar for the time of the interview and, I recommend, at least 15 minutes or more before, if possible. I realize that due to family or work demands this may not always be practical; however, if you can, that's great. I actually had a 3:00pm telephone interview scheduled once and the Recruiter called me at 2:30pm instead. I obviously did not point out her mistake but just went with it as, luckily, I had freed up my calendar. Even if the interviewer doesn't call 30 minutes early, these few extra minutes can give you time to review the job description or company website so everything is fresh in your mind or perhaps meditate for a few minutes so you're calm and ready to go when the time comes.

If you'll be participating in the telephone interview from home, ensure that you have a quiet place to take the call where you won't be interrupted. Background noises are sometimes unavoidable; however, control as much as you can to ensure no distractions for you or the interviewer during the call. This means, for example, have a family member or babysitter occupy the children or if you have a furry family member that likes to bark at the most inopportune times, is there someone who can take him/her for a walk? Most interviewers are understanding and forgiving of background noises; however, if at all possible, it's best to make this quiet, uninterrupted time.

Although the interviewer can't see you, you want to ensure you make a great first impression, so put a smile on your face and express enthusiasm in your voice (without going overboard). Such positive energy will travel through the phone lines and make a great impression on the interviewer. Even if you're not feeling very positive or enthusiastic that day, "Fake it 'til you Make it" as they say.

Video Interview – Preparing for a video interview is much like preparing for the telephone interview. There are a few additional things you'll want to take into account however. For example, the location. Do you have a home office from which you'll be doing the interview or will it be from your living room or dining room table? Any of these options are fine, but have a plan. Know, in advance, where you'll be doing the interview. Then check out the lighting, surroundings, etc.

With regard to lighting, ensure that your face won't be in the shadows. It's best to have the light source in the room coming from in front of you instead of behind you or from directly overhead. The light can be from a window, lamp, etc. Just think of it as if you're taking a photo. If the sun is behind the subject of the photo, then it's going to cast shadows or cause you to only see a silhouette of the subject.

Next, you want to look at the surrounding. What will the interviewer see in the background? I recommend having a blank wall or a wall with home décor of some type if possible but, honestly, most anything is fine as long as it's appropriate. You may be a really fun person who likes to party; however, the interviewer doesn't need to see the line of empty wine bottles on the kitchen counter. Nor would you want him/her to see a sink filled with dirty dishes or a laundry basket with your dirty underwear hanging over the side. Again, think about the impression you're making.

Also, think about the height of your webcam. For example, if you're tall and using the webcam on your laptop, you may want to set your laptop on a couple of books or something that will raise it up a bit. After all, you don't want to be looking down at it in such a way that the interviewer is looking up your nostrils throughout the entire interview.

In addition to considering your surroundings, you also want to plan what you're going to wear for your video interview. I recommend treating it just like a regular in-person interview and dressing appropriately. We've all seen YouTube videos of the person who dressed in a suit jacket & tie for a video interview or meeting but got caught wearing only his boxer shorts on the bottom. You don't want to end up in one of those videos, so dress appropriately top to bottom. After all, you never know what could happen that might cause you to have to move while the camera is still on. I share more about interview attire in the **In-Person Interview** section below; however, in this situation, I say better safe than sorry.

Finally, if possible, I highly recommend testing your laptop webcam and whatever program (WebEx, Zoom, HireVue, Skype, etc.) that will be used for your video interview in advance to ensure everything is working properly and the interview gets off to a great start. Interviews are stressful enough. No need to add to it by having to scramble at the last minute when you discover a technical difficulty. Also, you'll want to get familiar with the technology to ensure that you know how to connect, turn the video or audio on and off, etc. Again, just to ensure that things run smoothly and to reduce added stress.

In-Person Interview – There are several things to consider when preparing for an in-person interview. In addition to practice questions, etc. that I've described previously, I recommend the following:

- Go to bed early the night before so you're well-rested, fresh and energized for your interview.
- Ensure you have the correct address and know where you're supposed to go.
- Think about how long the commute is and the time of day. Will you be traveling in rush hour traffic that might add to your drive time?

- Plan to arrive 10-15 minutes before your interview.
- If you've never been to the location before, you may want to do a drive-by a day or two before to ensure you can find the address with no problem. Don't assume! Unexpected road construction, detours, a lack of street signs, etc. can easily mess you up on interview day.
- Bring 1 or 2 copies of your resume. The interviewers will most likely have their own copies; however, if by chance they don't, it's an opportunity to keep things moving and show them that you came prepared.

What to wear? As I mentioned in the **Video Interview** section above, it's an interview, so dress appropriately. Now this doesn't mean that you need to wear a three-piece suit; however, ensure you dress appropriately for the type of job for which you are interviewing. Even better, dress a step or two above. It's not a must; however, think about that first impression. For example, if a recruiter or hiring manager is interviewing for a warehouse employee and one candidate shows up for the interview in a T-shirt and jeans and another shows up in slacks, a tie and jacket…that makes an impression.

Why did I include this section? A colleague once had a candidate for a role show up in shorts and, during the interview, proceed to ask how long she would have to stay in that role before she could be promoted. She did NOT get the job!

CHAPTER THREE

The 3 C's of Interviewing

The 3 C's of Interviewing:
- Be Confident,
- Be Courteous (and Kind),
- Be Concise.

If you got the interview, you obviously have experience, skills and qualifications that are of interest to the prospective employer. Thus, ensure you keep things moving forward in a positive manner. The 3 C's will serve you well in this regard.

Be Confident:
This is not the time to be a shy wallflower. You don't want to go overboard and cross the line into arrogance however. As you proceed through the interview process, you want to ensure that the interviewer knows that you are confident in what you can bring to the table, yet humble enough to recognize that you don't know everything. Also, don't forget to smile and ensure that your posture, words and expressions reflect that you're a positive, energetic, results-oriented person that they will definitely want on their team.

Be Courteous & Kind:
Hopefully being courteous and kind toward others is part of your normal behavior; however, I also understand that we all have a bad day occasionally. Just be aware of things that set you off. If you're on edge about the interview because you desperately need the job or for any other reason, be conscious of this and don't let it get the best of you. As I've

said before "Fake it 'til you Make it". In all aspects of the interview process and even when traveling to/from the interview be courteous, kind and respectful of others at all times. After all, you never know who's watching (see the "Why did I include this section?" below).

Why did I include this section? Once, I flew a management candidate in and booked her into a local hotel the night before her interview. It just so happened that our new Plant Manager had been staying at this same hotel for several weeks while he started work and looked for a new home. In the process, he had gotten to know several members of the hotel staff, especially those who manned the front desk. Upon leaving the hotel the morning of the candidate's interview, he stopped by the front desk and the attendant shared with him that the candidate had been extremely rude and arrogant toward several members of the hotel staff. When he arrived at work, he immediately came to my office, told me about the candidate's behavior and was adamant that this was not the type of person he wanted on his team. Being that the candidate was scheduled to arrive very soon, we moved forward with the interview, but we all knew she had already lost the job.

Be Concise:
You want to be well prepared for your interview and have examples at the ready, but be careful not to ramble. Be thorough in your response, but be concise. Rambling can come off as unprofessional, and it can also cause you to say things that you later regret. Remember, listening is a great skill to have and one that many of us need to work on improving. Don't get caught in the trap of thinking about what you're going to say next rather than really listening to what the interviewer is asking. Being clear on what is being asked can help prevent you from rambling. Listen carefully and, if needed, take a few seconds to organize your thoughts before you speak. A few seconds of silence is okay…or a "Hmmm…let

me think of a good example" to buy yourself some time to formulate your response is perfectly fine.

Why did I include this section? Once, I brought a prospective candidate to my office for an interview and as soon as he sat down, he said, "Let me tell you about myself." Then, he proceeded to talk non-stop for the next 20 minutes. He did NOT get the job!

Finally, remember that the interview process is a two-way street. Not only is the employer interviewing you, but you should also be interviewing the employer. Not that you need to ask as many questions; however, during the process, some areas you may want to think about as you learn about the company and interact with those involved in the interview / hiring process include:

- Is this a company where I feel I will be happy?
- Does it seem that this role will challenge me and offer me opportunities to advance?
- Does the company offer the benefits, etc. that are important to me?
- Do I feel that I will fit in with the culture of the company?
- Has anything of concern come up during the interview process? *(This may be that little voice we all have inside us. If something is making you uncomfortable about working for the company, listen to your gut. After the interview, take time to think it through and see if you can put your finger on just what's bothering you, but don't just ignore it. That little voice is there to help you.)*
- If there is something about the job that you are unclear about, ask for clarification.

CHAPTER FOUR

After the Interview

Immediate "To Do":

As soon as possible after the interview, send a thank you note. This can be via email if you have the email addresses of those who interviewed you or you can go old school and mail handwritten "Thank You" notes. This may seem outdated; however, it is appreciated and shows that you went the extra mile and did something that took a little more effort than just a quick email.

Follow Up:

Hopefully, the interview process moves quickly; however, unfortunately, that is not always the case. Hiring decisions can be delayed for all sorts of reasons that may have absolutely nothing to do with you. Patience may be a little more challenging for some of us than others; however, just remember…patience is a virtue (allegedly).

There's nothing wrong with following up though. If you asked during the interview when you should expect to hear back and were given a timeframe, for example, if you were told that it would be at least two weeks before you heard back, then wait the allotted time. Otherwise, I recommend after a week or so, if you haven't heard anything, call or email your contact for an update. This follow up can be done via email or telephone and might go something like the following:

Dear (name of contact),

I hope you are doing well and having a great week. I thoroughly enjoyed meeting you and the rest of the hiring team during my interview on (date) and thought I would check in to see if there are any updates.

I'm very interested in working at (name of Company) and hope to hear from you soon.

Best regards,

If for some reason you don't hear back, wait another week and follow up again. Perhaps via a different method this time (i.e., if you sent an email the first time, pick up the telephone and call this time.) It could be that your email got buried in the individual's in-box or accidentally went to his/her spam folder.

CONCLUSION

I sincerely hope that you have found these recommendations informative and helpful. Although every interview may not be successful, we set ourselves up for greater possibilities of success if we make the effort to be well prepared from the start.

> *"By failing to prepare, you are preparing to fail."*
> *- Benjamin Franklin*

Best wishes and an abundance of blessings to you and your family!

ABOUT THE AUTHOR

Monica Boitnott has approximately 20 years of experience in Human Resources and has worked in multiple industries. She obtained her MBA from Auburn University in Auburn, AL and also has a Bachelor's of Arts degree in Organizational Communication from Queens College in Charlotte, NC. Additionally, she obtained her SPHR (Senior Professional in Human Resources) certification from the Human Resources Certification Institute in 2010. Over the years, she has been involved in the recruiting and interviewing process for literally hundreds of job openings. She has also conducted numerous training sessions related to hiring and interviewing best practices, has advised individuals on how to prepare their resumes, and coached many on how to put their best foot forward during the job search process.

Made in the USA
Coppell, TX
05 August 2020